A ROOKIE READER

JUST LIKE ME

By Barbara J. Neasi

Illustrations by Lois Axeman

Prepared under the direction of Robert Hillerich, Ph.D.

CHILDRENS PRESS ™

CHICAGO

To Jennifer and Julie

Library of Congress Cataloging in Publication Data

Neasi, Barbara J.
  Just like me.

  Summary: A little girl describes all the things she
and her twin sister have in common.
  [1. Twins—Fiction.   2. Sisters—Fiction] I. Axeman,
  Lois, ill.   II. Title.
PZ7.N295Ju 1984   [E]   83-23154
ISBN 0-516-02047-1

17 18 19 20 R 99 98

My name is Jennifer.
I have a twin sister.
Her name is Julie.

She has long brown hair.
Just like me!

She has big brown eyes.
Just like me!

6

Julie is in first grade.
Just like me!

She goes to dance class.

Just like me!

She likes to roller skate.

Just like me!

She likes bubble gum.
Just like me!

13

She sleeps in a big bed.

Just like me!

Julie has a kitten.

Not like me!

She likes to clean house.
Not like me!

Julie likes to float on the water.

Not like me!

She likes to wear dresses.
Not like me!

She likes pancakes.
Not like me!

Julie likes to wear black shoes.

Not like me!

Julie wakes up early.

Not like me!

Sometimes we are the same.
Sometimes we are different.
But we are always twin sisters!

WORD LIST

a	early	is	same
always	eyes	Jennifer	she
are	first	Julie	shoes
bed	float	just	sister(s)
big	goes	kitten	skate
black	grade	like(s)	sleeps
brown	gum	long	sometimes
bubble	hair	me	the
but	has	my	to
class	have	name	twin
clean	her	not	up
dance	house	on	wakes
different	I	pancakes	water
dresses	in	roller	we
			wear

About the Author

Barbara Neasi is a writer and the mother of twin daughters. She wrote this book because she found there was a lack of suitable material describing how twins can look the same and like the same things but in many other ways they are very different. This is the first book she has had published by Childrens Press.

About the Artist

Lois Axeman was born and raised in Chicago, Illinois. She studied art in Chicago at the American Academy, Illinois Institute of Technology, and at the Art Institute. She taught illustration at the University of Illinois Circle Campus for four years. The mother of two grown children and grandmother of one, Lois and her husband, Harvey Retzloff, live on the fifty-fourth floor of a lakefront building where they both pursue their careers in the graphic arts. They share their home with their Shih Tzu dog Marty and their female cat Charlie. Lois uses her children, her grandchild, and her pets as models for her picture book characters. In their spare time Lois and Harvey enjoy painting, playing tennis, and growing orchids.